IS-454: Fundamentals of Risk Management

By

Fema

10/31/2013

IS-454: Fundamentals of Risk Management

Table of Contents:

About the Course

This course will introduce the essential role of risk management at the Department of Homeland Security (DHS). As a member of the DHS workforce, it is imperative that you have a general awareness of the concept of risk management and its applications to homeland security and your job within the Department.

As you will learn in the coming lessons, everyone manages risk. The more structured approach that we call "risk management" gives us a logical process for identifying potential risks, deciding what to do about them, and then doing it.

This course will introduce the essential role of risk management at the Department of Homeland Security (DHS). As a member of the DHS workforce, it is imperative that you have a general awareness of the concept of risk management and its applications to homeland security and your individual job.

By developing your understanding of the principles of risk management, you will enhance your ability to contribute to DHS and its unified effort to manage risks to the Nation from a diverse and complex set of threats and hazards. These include, but are not limited to, but are not limited to natural disasters, human error, terrorism, cyber threats, crime, and security and safety issues.

By the end of this course, you will be able to:

- Recognize the value of risk management.
- Explain how the fundamental concepts and principles of risk management apply at home, in the workplace, and in the community.
- Explain how the DHS Risk Management Cycle utilizes logical reasoning and critical thinking to address risk management problems.

- Describe how risk management alternatives are developed and evaluated in order to support making better decisions that will effectively manage risk.
- Explain how and why the management of risk is one of the fundamental strategies adopted by DHS in meeting mission performance expectations.
- Describe the characteristics of effective risk communication.

Lesson 1: Introduction to Risk Management

The Value of Risk Management

Risk is something all of us encounter, whether we are in our homes, at work, or on the go.

Dealing with risk is an everyday part of life. It is not some "special" activity that relates to only particular people with certain jobs. We all manage risk.

At the Department of Homeland Security, risk management occupies an essential role in our unified effort to protect the Nation from a diverse and complex set of threats and hazards.

As members of the DHS workforce, it is vital that we understand the fundamental concepts of risk management.

By familiarizing ourselves with the principles and processes of effectively managing risk, we will more clearly understand our individual roles in the homeland security effort.

Screen Features

- Click the **Exit** button to close this window and exit the course.
- Click the **Course Menu** button to access the menu listing all lessons of this course. You can select any of the lessons from this menu by simply clicking on the lesson title.
- Click the **Glossary** button to look up key definitions and acronyms.
- Click the **Help** button to review guidance and troubleshooting advice regarding navigating through the course.
- Track your progress by looking at the **Progress** bar at the top right of each screen. To see a numeric display, roll your mouse over the Progress bar area.
- Follow the **bolded instructions** that appear on each screen in order to proceed to the next screen or complete a Knowledge Review or Activity.
- Click the **left** or **right arrows** at the top and bottom of screens to move backward or forward in the lesson. Note: If the right arrow button is disabled, you must complete an activity before you can proceed in the lesson.

Navigating Using Your Keyboard

Below are instructions for navigating through the course using your keyboard.

- Use the "Tab" key to move forward through each screen's navigation buttons and hyperlinks, or "Shift" + "Tab" to move backwards. A box surrounds the button that is currently selected.
- Press "Enter" to select a navigation button or hyperlink.
- Use the arrow keys to select answers for multiple-choice review questions or self-assessment checklists. Then tab to the "Submit" button and press "Enter" to complete a Knowledge Review or Self-Assessment.
- Warning: Repeatedly pressing "Tab" beyond the number of selections on the screen may cause the keyboard to lock up. Use "Ctrl" + "Tab" to deselect an element or reset to the beginning of a screen's navigation links (most often needed for screens with animations or media).
- JAWS assistive technology users can press the Ctrl key to quiet the screen reader while the course audio plays.

Receiving Credit

To receive credit for this course, you will need to complete the final exam with a minimum score of 75%. The last screen in this course provides instructions on how to complete the final exam.

NOTE: Try to complete each lesson in one sitting. If you exit from the course before completing a lesson, you will have to start that lesson over again. The length of each lesson is on the Lesson Overview Screen.

Lesson Overview

In this lesson you will learn about the value of risk management. It is important to understand this value and how the concepts of risk management apply to both your personal life and to the roles and responsibilities you fulfill at DHS.

There are several principles and concepts underlying the practice of risk management which are fundamental to managing all kinds of risks. At the end of the day, it is what we do or don't do about a given risk that determines how we are affected by it. A sound understanding of this connection will allow you to recognize and use risk management processes throughout the day-to-day business of DHS.

Upon completion of this lesson, you will be able to:

- Describe the value of risk management to your personal life, workplace, and community.

Risk Management in Real Life

Hi there! My name is Bob and I'll be sharing some of my own risk management experiences with you throughout this course. Have you noticed that there seems to be a lot of talk about natural disasters in the news lately?

Over the past couple of years, there always seems to be something in the news about flooding, hurricanes, snowstorms, earthquakes, tornados…you name it.

During an ice storm that hit my area last winter, we lost power for almost 48 hours. We were lucky, though. Some people had no electricity for over a week! Anyway, my wife and I started talking about the possibility of buying a backup generator for our home.

Losing electricity in that storm last winter caused us a lot of headaches. My wife had to miss work, the water line to our kitchen sink froze, and we had to move food out of the refrigerator to keep it from spoiling. Thanks to some help from our neighbors, everything turned out okay.

Since then, my mother moved in with us so we could help take care of her. Mom's health is pretty frail at times and I'm not sure what I would do if we lost power again.

So, we've been weighing the pros and cons of getting a generator. A good one costs quite a bit and times are tight. They also need gas and upkeep and can be dangerous if you don't know what you're doing.

On the other hand, my mom wouldn't do too well without heat in the house and some of her medications have to be refrigerated. I also worry about those pipes freezing up and possibly bursting.

I just keep thinking about the possibility of another one of those storms and being prepared as much as possible sounds like a good idea. Today, I've found a good generator on sale and we need to make a decision. But how?

What is Risk?

Risk is something that we encounter and must deal with in almost every aspect of our lives. Whether we are at home, at work, or on the go, some type of risk is always present. But what exactly is risk?

In simple terms, risk is the potential for an unwanted outcome. The key words here are "potential" and "unwanted." These words relate well to two additional terms that we hear quite often when learning about risk: likelihood and consequences.

Likelihood is the chance (or potential) of something happening; consequences are the unwanted effect of an event, incident, or occurrence.

Risk Assessment and Risk Management

The terms likelihood and consequences become very important as we begin to look at risk and think more about how it affects us at home and in the workplace. By thinking about risk (whether we are doing that intentionally or subconsciously), we soon find ourselves engaging in what is known as <u>risk assessment</u>. That is, we begin to consider the likelihood and consequences of particular risks.

Thinking about risks in terms of how likely they are to happen and what their consequences might be is a key part of managing them. In general, risk management is the process of identifying and assessing a risk, developing and analyzing alternative courses of action, deciding what to do about that risk (including the possibility of deliberately doing nothing), and then doing it. Effective management of risk cannot happen without some type of risk assessment.

Risk Assessment

Risk assessment often involves considering these three questions:

1. What can happen?
2. How likely is it to happen?
3. What are the consequences if it does happen?

Adapted from *On the Quantitative Definition of Risk* by Stanley Kaplan and John Garrick: http://onlinelibrary.wiley.com/doi/10.1111/j.1539-6924.1981.tb01350.x/abstract

Assessing Risk

Assessing risk and then developing and analyzing alternative courses of action can be a very involved process requiring specialized expertise and considerable time and effort to accomplish. It can also be done very quickly and informally. In fact, it can be almost instinctive.

Think about a law enforcement officer making an entry into a potentially hostile environment or facing a "shoot/don't shoot" situation. Law enforcement officers are trained to rapidly assess situations, develop alternatives, and make a choice. They frequently have to act quickly on their own, while processing all the necessary factors in their heads. You may not have thought of it this way before, but in doing these kinds of things, law enforcement officers practice risk management continuously while they are on the job. Similar tasks carried out every day by other homeland security professionals incorporate similar risk management elements.

Risk Management in Real Life

You can see how my decision on whether or not to buy a generator involves risk assessment.

I understand that we are dealing with the risk of losing power and have a pretty good idea of the possible consequences since it has already happened to us before.

For me, the hardest part is figuring out how likely it will be for this to happen again. I'm sure there will be another storm, but I don't know if that will be next year or in ten years!

The Value of Risk Management

Risk management is an everyday part of life. It is not some "special" activity that relates to only particular people with certain jobs. It is applicable to everyone in all sorts of ways and can happen consciously or unconsciously. Even if this is the first time you have read anything about risk or likelihood and consequences, you still have a great deal of personal experience in managing risk.

The value of deliberate risk management comes from handling risk in a planned way instead of just accepting or allowing consequences of events to affect you without forethought or preparation.

Consider these additional points about the value of managing risk:

- Risk management is a way of dealing with problems encountered at home or on the job; it is not an end in and of itself.
- Risk management is part of sound organizational practices that include planning, preparedness, program evaluation, process improvement, budget priority development and, most importantly, operational execution in the field.
- The value of a risk management approach or strategy to decision-makers or operators is providing various approaches or options in managing risks.

Managing Risk at Home

Risk management is a method for approaching problems in all aspects of life, including many of the situations we encounter at home or in our personal lives. Do you lock the door to your home whenever you leave? Most of us do because we have identified the risks of leaving our home unlocked. There is some level of likelihood that someone could enter that door and steal our valuables. By locking the door, we have taken a risk management action and reduced the potential for an unwanted consequence.

Of course, we don't all manage risk in the same way and there are a variety of reasons for this. Deciding on a risk management action such as locking your door or buying a generator often depends upon a number of factors that can affect how we view risks. We will talk about these more in the next lesson.

Managing Risk in the Community

Risk management is something we often see in our own communities. There are many risks to the public at large, and our various levels of government spend a good deal of time trying to identify those. Once risks are identified in the community, many factors go into the process of deciding if something could or should be done and exactly how to do that.

This is why communities adopt a range of prevention, protection, mitigation, response, and recovery measures. These can include supporting police and fire departments, requiring permits and inspections for construction and other activities, implementing neighborhood watch groups, installing traffic lights, and developing local emergency response plans for events such as hurricanes and chemical spills.

As citizens, we play a vital risk management role in the community. For instance, we can help identify new risks as they emerge. This is the idea behind the "If You See Something, Say SomethingTM" public awareness campaign which emphasizes the importance of reporting suspicious activity to the proper authorities.

Another way we can help with risk management in the community is by being prepared for known hazards and threats. The Ready.gov website outlines how being informed and prepared for potential emergencies can benefit us as individuals and as a community.

You are encouraged to go to www.ready.gov to learn more.

Managing Risk in the Workplace

Our involvement in risk management doesn't stop when we enter the workplace. In fact, it often becomes even more important, regardless of where we work. A primary reason for this is that our involvement with risk management at work usually has consequences or effects on others besides ourselves. It can also have many different types of consequences.

As the stakes are often higher and the risks tend to be more complex in the workplace, it becomes more important for us to understand the risk management processes in that environment. In the workplace, we are usually required to manage risk at the organizational level rather than our own personal level. Relying on informal or instinctive risk management may not be effective since we need to view likelihood and consequences from an organizational level or perspective and not just our own.

Types of Consequences

There are many different consequences for risks encountered in the workplace and those can be categorized in several ways. Each type of consequence listed below could be illustrated with many specific examples. For instance, a poor decision might cause a company to suffer the economic consequences of losing sales revenue.

- Economic
- Human
- Mission
- Psychological

Risk Management in the Department of Homeland Security (DHS)

DHS has a major responsibility as one of many important risk managers for the nation. This is especially true because of the Department's role in the larger national homeland security enterprise. DHS is required to work effectively with risk managers in other agencies, in other levels of government, and in the private sector, and has an obligation to lead by example.

It is vital that everyone at every level within the DHS workforce has a fundamental understanding of risk management so that risk management becomes a permanent part of our DHS culture.

Customs and Border Protection Agent:

As a Customs and Border Protection Agent, I see the implications of risk management on a daily basis. But I think a great example of risk management in action at DHS came on a recent Super Bowl Sunday.

Even before the final seconds ticked away on the Super Bowl, DHS components and employees made sure that the final score for security at the nation's biggest football game was never in doubt.

As with previous Super Bowls, a combined DHS/FBI Team worked closely with partners at the federal, state and local levels several months in advance to help secure the venue.

The risk management objective was to ensure the safety and security of fans, players, officials, news media and dignitaries who attended or participated in the event.

NPPD's Office of Infrastructure Protection, Super Bowl team of two Regional Directors and nine Protective Security Advisors conducted 32 vulnerability assessments on key event venues and supporting infrastructure before the game.

ICE Homeland Security Investigation agents partnered with local police and the FBI on Crime Action Teams, were members of Visible Intermodal Protection and Response teams, and supplied a Mobile Command Center near the stadium.

CBP's Office of Air and Marine brought in AW-139 and AS-350 helicopters and Cessna C-550 Citation II airplanes, along with pilots and crew members, to monitor airspace; secure the game day temporary flight restriction; and feed live video from air surveillance to local law enforcement on the ground.

S&T provided nearly 100 multi-band radios to police, rescue agencies, and members of the FBI and National Guard to allow these agencies who normally use different radio bands, to communicate without further aid. S&T also provided a suite of risk management tools that allow incident commanders to capture details about an incident or suspicious activity and incorporate that into the total risk picture.

TSA provided First Observer awareness training for more than 8,000 transportation, hospitality, security and volunteer workers and deployed Visible Intermodal Protection and Response teams to support transportation security.

Through its BioWatch Program, the DHS Office of Health Affairs deployed collectors at the stadium and nearby convention center.

Four FEMA Region V Liaison Officers were deployed to support 24/7 operations and FEMA also supported the state Emergency Operations Center, which maintained awareness and ensured operational capability.
Of course, this was just one event. But it shows how risk management can involve many different DHS Components and personnel at many different levels.

Risk Management Applications

Managing risk is an essential function of homeland security and everyone's responsibility at DHS. Employees of DHS Components work to identify, understand, and address the complex challenges and opportunities encountered in our various roles.

Consider the following issues, functions, or areas of management concern which can benefit from the conscientious application of risk management principles and processes.

- Strategic Planning
- Capabilities-based Planning
- Resource Decisions
- Operational Planning
- Exercise Planning
- Real-world Events
- Research and Development

Strategic Planning

Addresses risks that an organization faces, taking a long-term view to building risk management programs and capabilities through prevention, protection, response, and recovery activities.

Capabilities-based Planning

Planning under uncertainty to provide capabilities suitable for a wide range of modern-day challenges and circumstances while working within an economic framework that necessitates choice.

Resource Decisions

Key components of an information-driven approach to requesting and allocating resources, including grant funding.

Operational Planning

Identifies the risk-reducing objectives to be addressed by the planned operation. For example, identifying contraband and preventing it from entering the nation or locating a vessel in distress and rendering appropriate aid.

Also identifies risks that might be encountered by those carrying out the operation and how to deal with such risks. For example, a booby-trap in a hidden compartment or weather and sea conditions beyond the safe operating limits of a particular rescue craft.

Exercise Planning

Identifies realistic scenarios for exercises, zeroing in on threats and hazards, priority capabilities, and applicable assets.

Real-world Events

Involves weighing potential courses of action within a contextual understanding of the risk posed by the situation at hand, whether routine in nature or during an emergency.

Research and Development

Informs decisions on actions to fill capability gaps that require technology beyond the current state of the art, to close gaps in available knowledge, or to improve existing effectiveness and/or efficiency through new technology or knowledge.

Risk Management in Real Life

The more we understand risk management the more we discover what a valuable tool it can be. My decision on whether or not to purchase a generator was based on some common risk management principles that we all practice from day to day. What would you choose to do in this situation?

In my situation, we were trying to manage the risk and consequences of losing power again against the cost of buying a new generator. We considered the likelihood of another storm and had to weigh the consequences of not having electricity against the expense of a generator.

Choosing between going without electricity or having to spend that extra money was not an easy decision. We had to evaluate all the options in the context of what was most important to us and it was helpful to have a framework in which to make that decision.

After talking it over, we decided that, for our circumstances, being without a generator was not worth the risk. While we considered taking some more affordable precautions, like getting a kerosene heater and stocking up on emergency supplies, knowing that a lack of electricity would make it difficult to take care of my mother determined our course of action.

Lesson Summary

In this lesson you learned about risk management and its value in the home, the community, and in the workplace.

Managing risk is something that we do every day. Risk management concepts and principles provide a logical and disciplined way of identifying, understanding, and dealing with problems including the consideration of available alternative solutions, whether in our personal lives or on the job.

In our next lesson, we will learn more about the concepts of risk management and move toward understanding how to apply those in decision-making.

Lesson 2: Basic Risk Management Concepts

Lesson Overview

This lesson will provide the basic concepts and principles of risk management that you can apply at home, in the community, and in the workplace. Gaining an understanding of key terminology will make you better prepared to understand risk management as a whole.

You will also learn about different types of risk and the influence of risk perception on decision-making as you practice recognizing the role of risk management in various situations.

Upon completion of this lesson, you will be able to:

- Recall basic risk terminology.
- Describe the fundamental concepts of risk management.
- Describe the key principles for effective risk management.
- Explain the role of risk management principles in dealing with a given situation or problem.

Risk Management in Real Life

Hello, again! The last time I talked to you I had just purchased a backup generator for my home. I haven't needed it so far but it does feel good knowing it will be ready if and when the time comes.

Speaking of "being ready," I started to think about other ways that my family could be prepared for an emergency and decided to take a look at the Ready.gov website.

The website had information and instructions on making an emergency plan and building a disaster supplies kit.

As I looked over this information I saw there were several things in the supplies kit list that I had not considered before, but I realized would be very necessary.

Later, I sat down with my family and we talked about making a plan and gathering the supplies for a kit.

My daughter drew a connection to her participation in the emergency drills at her school. She also had lots of questions about how she would contact us if an emergency happened during the day when we were at work.

I wanted my daughter to know that by taking these steps now, in advance, we would be better prepared for any future emergency when time and resources could be limited. Like doing your homework before the weekend is over, so there's no big rush.

Risk Management in Real Life

What are your experiences with emergency planning at home? Does your household have an emergency plan or emergency supplies kit?

Note: Building or purchasing an emergency kit requires little time and can be done using readily available supplies at home. While building or purchasing an emergency kit is optional and cannot be reimbursed, it is highly encouraged.

Part of me felt like this was overkill and there would probably never be a need for us to use a kit or put an emergency plan into effect. My wife and I even worried that there was a chance it would make our kids paranoid about some type of disaster.

But, discussing it with them convinced me that we had far more to lose by not being prepared. We agreed as a family to work on an emergency plan and kit in the coming weeks and I'm glad we are going ahead with this.

Risk Management Terminology

As we discuss managing risk in more detail, it will be necessary to have a sound understanding of the related terminology. The following terms are used often in this course. By selecting the term, you can view the definition as provided in the *DHS Risk Lexicon, 2010 Edition.*

In other points throughout the lessons, we will sometimes present explanations of these terms using slightly different language. However, those instances are not intended to suggest a definition different from those presented here.

- Risk
- Risk Management
- Hazard
- Threat
- Vulnerability
- Likelihood
- Consequence
- Risk Perception

Risk

The potential for an unwanted outcome resulting from an incident, event, or occurrence, as determined by its likelihood and the associated consequences.

Risk Management

The process of identifying, analyzing, assessing, and communicating risk and accepting, avoiding, transferring or controlling it to an acceptable level considering associated costs and benefits of any action taken.

(In this course, risk management is defined more simply as a process for identifying the potential for an unwanted outcome, determining what to do about it from among the available alternatives, and then doing it.)

Hazard

A natural or man-made source of harm or difficulty.

(In this course, hazard is generally used to indicate sources of harm where there is no deliberate intent such as a natural disaster, accidental hazmat spill, etc.)

Threat

A natural or man-made occurrence, individual, entity, or action that has or indicates the potential to harm life, information, operations, the environment, and /or property.

(For the purposes of this course, threat generally refers to an intentional act with the potential to cause harm; a terrorist attack, for example.)

Vulnerability

A physical feature or operational attribute that renders an entity, asset, system, network, or geographic area open to exploitation or susceptible to a given hazard.

Likelihood

The chance of something happening, described in either quantitative terms of probability or frequency, or in qualitative terms.

For example:

- The probability of "heads" appearing when flipping a coin is 50%.
- Frequency could be described as, "on average, there are serious automobile accidents at this intersection 12 times each year."
- A qualitative likelihood could be expressed in terms such as rare, almost certain, as likely as not.

Consequence

The effect of an event, incident, or occurrence including, but not limited to, death or injury, property damage, business loss, and psychological effects. Consequences can be evaluated without consideration for the likelihood of the event or our ability to prevent or mitigate the effect.

Risk Perception

Subjective beliefs and/or judgments about the characteristics and/or severity of risk.

Risk Management Concepts

There are a number of risk management concepts that are important to our discussions here. Consider the following when you think about managing risk:

- **Risk management is how we approach problems to minimize the negative impact we suffer from their existence.** The idea is that by correctly applying this approach, we should enhance our organization's overall decision-making process and maximize its ability to achieve its objectives.
- **Risk can be shaped and controlled, but it usually cannot be eliminated.** Resource considerations may lead us to a decision to accept that risk. Risk acceptance is something we will discuss more when we address risk management strategies.
- **Risk is managed at many different levels.** We learned a little about this when we discussed how to apply risk management at home or in the workplace. Regardless of whether we are managing risk informally at home or as part of a formal process at work, the same higher level concepts and principles apply. The basic steps we need to take in applying these risk management concepts and principles are also the same, although the specific details and the degree of formality will vary depending on circumstances.

Risk Management:

The process of identifying, analyzing, assessing, and communicating risk and accepting, avoiding, transferring or controlling it to an acceptable level considering associated costs and benefits of any action taken.

Risk Management Principles

Risk management allows us to do many things. At DHS, it enables us to distinguish between and among alternative actions, assess our capabilities, and prioritize activities and resources. In order to manage risk effectively, there are certain key principles that we must follow:

- <u>Unity of Effort</u>
- <u>Transparency</u>
- <u>Adaptability</u>
- <u>Practicality</u>
- <u>Customization</u>

Unity of Effort

Risk management efforts should be coordinated and integrated among all partners. Most homeland security activities involve representatives of different organizations and it is important that there is unity of effort among those charged with managing risks, even if there isn't unity of command.

Transparency

A principle of risk management emphasizing the importance of providing clear and unambiguous information regarding all processes throughout the risk management effort that helps establish trust with stakeholders.

Adaptability

Risk management actions, strategies, and processes should be designed to remain dynamic and responsive to change. Operating in a constantly evolving landscape, DHS and its homeland security partners must be flexible in their approach to managing risk.

Practicality

Even the most sophisticated risk management cannot eliminate all uncertainty nor be reasonably expected to identify all risks and their likelihood and consequences. Despite the importance and effectiveness of the risk management approach, there are limitations that must be considered.

Another dimension of practicality relates to the costs of risk management efforts, as well as the costs of performing analyses, etc. It does not make sense to spend millions of dollars to assess a one-hundred thousand dollar risk.

Finally, there is the issue of time. In the case of time-critical decisions such as an emergency response, the time factor limits the amount of analysis that can be performed, regardless of the potential consequences of the risk and decision.

Customization

There is no one method to assess, analyze, respond to, or communicate about risk. The methods used in a given situation or dealing with a given problem must be tailored to the characteristics of that situation or problem, as well as to the responsibilities and information needs of the decision-maker, the expectations of stakeholders, etc. However, the need to customize does not supersede or eliminate the need to adhere to organizational standards, requirements and operating procedures.

Types of Risk

There are a number of different ways to categorize risk. One way to distinguish risks facing any organization is to divide them into either <u>internal or external risks</u>. Organizations should implement comprehensive risk management approaches to ensure both internal and external risks are considered in a holistic way.

Additionally, as an organization establishes a comprehensive approach to risk management, it can use the following organizational risk categories.

- <u>Strategic</u>
- <u>Operational</u>
- <u>Institutional</u>

Internal or External

This classification considers both where the risk arises and where the effects of the risk are felt. Examples of internal sources of risk include issues such as financial stewardship, personnel reliability, and systems reliability. All organizations are subject to these types of internal risk.

DHS exists to manage risks on behalf of the American public. An internal risk may affect the ability of DHS to meet its objectives but that failure could ultimately affect the American populace, whether the failure resulted in a major cost overrun of taxpayer dollars or a failed disaster response.

External sources of risk include global, political, and societal trends, as well as hazards from natural disasters, terrorism, malicious activity, and manmade accidents. It is important that external threats remain at the forefront of consideration for homeland security organizations since managing these risks on behalf of the American people is why DHS exists.

Strategic

In the homeland security and national security contexts, strategic risk can have three meanings. These are risks that can affect:

1. Vital national interests, such as preservation of our core values and system of governance.

2. An organization's vital interests, such as building a reputation for operational effectiveness or as good
3. Successful execution of a chosen strategy.

Strategic risks can be imposed by external threats, such as the natural environment or human actors, or they can arise from flawed or poorly implemented strategy, as well as from ineffective management.

In the first level of meaning, managing strategic risks to vital national interests that arise in the homeland security arena is why DHS and its partner agencies exist. At the second and third levels of meaning, strategic risks threaten the Department's ability to successfully execute its strategy, as well as position itself to recognize, anticipate, and respond to future trends, conditions, and challenges. Strategic risks include those factors that may impact the organization's overall objectives and long-term goals.

Operational

Operational risks have the potential to impede the successful execution of operations with existing resources, capabilities, and strategies.

These risks include those that impact personnel, time, materials, equipment, tactics, techniques, information, technology, and procedures that enable an organization to achieve its mission objectives.

Institutional

Institutional risks are associated with an organization's ability to develop and maintain effective management practices, control systems, and flexibility and adaptability to meet organizational requirements.

These risks are less obvious and typically come from within an organization. They can include factors that threaten an organization's ability to organize, recruit, train, support, and integrate the organization to meet all specified operational and administrative requirements.

Risk Perception

Your answers in the activity just presented were most likely affected by your perceptions of certain risks. Risk perception affects everyone and it is a critical facet of managing risk.

When you go to the beach, are you more concerned about shark attacks or heat exhaustion? What about developing skin cancer from overexposure to sunlight? All of these are risks, but the perception of the likelihood and consequences of each risk varies greatly depending upon the individual. For instance, someone who has had skin cancer previously is likely to perceive that risk as higher than either the shark attack or heat exhaustion; however, someone who spends a lot of time outside but has no knowledge of the actual risk of shark attacks may perceive the shark attack as a higher risk.

Risk perception is a critical element that can both drive the risk management process and be affected by it. Risk perception based solely on subjective, psychological responses to a certain threat will likely result in poor decision-making. Conversely, recognizing that an uninformed perception may be wrong and working to develop a realistic understanding based on objective assessment and analysis is a fundamental part of good risk management.

Finally, understanding that others may perceive risks differently than you do can help you communicate more effectively with them about those risks.

Why Manage Risk?

At this point, it is important that you have an understanding of why we manage risk. There are many reasons we could list, but the following provide a helpful outline.

- We manage risk in order to minimize the harm we suffer from the consequences of risk. The harm in question could be deaths, injuries, property destruction or economic loss due to external hazards or threats. However, harm could also result from ill-considered actions and ineffective programs and spending intended to address risk.
- Risk management practices help protect and enhance our personal and organizational interests by mitigating or avoiding the effects of risks while also helping to ensure that the things we do in response to risk make sense and are effective.
- Risk management enables us to distinguish between and among alternative actions and make it more likely that we will choose wise courses of action.
- Within the DHS environment, where there are constraints on resources, data, and time, risk management serves as a useful approach for weighing options and selecting the most appropriate course of action.

Risk Management in Real Life

Hello. A few minutes ago I shared my experience with preparing an emergency plan for my family. That type of planning and preparation is a good example of the risk management concepts you just learned.

The planning we did as a family represented a process of decision-making in which we assessed certain risks, their likelihood and consequences, and decided what to do about them. Of course, our planning is not intended to eliminate risk but rather to control the consequences whenever we can.

Making an emergency plan and supplies kit also demonstrated risk management principles discussed in this lesson. Our family discussions and participation highlighted a unity of effort and transparency.

As we continue to work on our plans we will need to show adaptability in our decision making, choosing practical decisions and customizing the plan to our needs.

One other aspect that tied into our emergency planning was risk perception. Even within our household, we don't all look at certain risks the same way.

Some people might never consider making an emergency plan since they just can't perceive those risks as being great enough. I guess my job has made me see things and think about them a little differently.

Lesson Summary

In this lesson, you learned about the basic concepts and principles of risk management including basic risk management terminology. You also learned about different ways to categorize risk.

An understanding of the key principles for basic risk management and the influence of risk perception, prepares you to actively apply those principles in a decision-making process.

Lesson 3: The DHS Risk Management Cycle (Part 1)

Lesson Overview

In this lesson you will learn about the DHS Risk Management Cycle and how it allows you to effectively manage risk.

You will also gain specific details about the first three steps of the DHS Risk Management Cycle:

1. Define the context
2. Identify potential risk
3. Assess and analyze risk

By understanding the overall risk cycle and having a more detailed knowledge of these first steps, you will be a better risk manager and decision-maker.

Upon completion of this lesson, you will be able to:

- Describe the DHS Risk Management Cycle.
- List potential sources of risk information.
- Recognize the elements of a particular risk (likelihood and consequence) in a given scenario.

Risk Management in Real Life

Hello, again. Today you have found me at my job as a Transportation Security Officer with the Transportation Security Administration (TSA).

I have been working with TSA for eight years now. We face a lot of challenges everyday as we work to protect the nation's transportation systems and make them safe for everyone.

Just like my decisions to purchase a generator and make an emergency plan at home, we make a lot of decisions at TSA to manage risks that we encounter. Risk management is an extremely important part of our job that plays a major role in decisions that affect millions of people.

Just take airport security for example. How do you feel about going through the security screening process at airports? Not many people enjoy the inconvenience of measures to screen passengers and their luggage.

However, these standard measures all represent an effort to manage risk. Read some more about the DHS Risk Management Cycle, and then I'll explain further.

The DHS Risk Management Cycle

In order to develop standard practices for risk management, a group of risk experts drawn from every element and Component of the Department developed the DHS Risk Management Cycle (Risk Management Fundamentals, 2011). The cycle promotes comparability and a shared understanding of information and analysis in the process. Ultimately, the risk management cycle facilitates better structured and informed decision-making.

The DHS Risk Management Cycle and You

As we begin to take a closer look at the DHS Risk Management Cycle, it is important to think about what this process means to you. First, you should understand that although the cycle promotes a careful and deliberate approach to risk management, you might often apply its concepts in a more informal method. This will largely depend upon the types of risks being addressed.

It is also likely that you could be involved with only part of the DHS Risk Management Cycle. Often, you might be part of implementing a policy or action that was developed by following the steps described in the Risk Management Cycle. Regardless of how involved you are with the particular steps of the cycle, you will benefit by understanding its essential role throughout DHS and how those principles apply to your individual roles at work and at home.

Define the Context

To manage risk it is critical that the risk manager/decision-maker understands and defines the context that the risk management effort will address. Risk managers and analysts need to have a thorough understanding of the environment in which the identified risks will be managed, including the requirements, constraints, and assumptions that will affect risk management actions. Defining the context informs and shapes all of the successive stages of the risk management cycle.

To better understand this first step of the cycle, consider how the risk manager/decision-maker would answer the following questions?

- What are my risk management responsibilities?
- What is my risk management environment?
- What outcomes and objectives am I expected to achieve?

Of course, if you are the responsible risk manager/decision-maker, you can answer these questions for yourself. If, however, you are supporting a risk manager/decision-maker, that individual is the one responsible for answering these questions. Finding out that person's perspective is an important element of the larger risk communications task that will be talked about in a later lesson.

Key Considerations for Defining the Context

When the context of a formal risk management effort is being defined, there are a number of considerations that should be identified and understood.

- Goals and Objectives
- Mission Space and Values
- Policies and Standards
- Scope and Criticality of the Decision
- Decision Makers and Stakeholders
- Decision Timeframe
- Risk Management Capabilities and Resources
- Risk Tolerance

Goals and Objectives

The goals and objectives being pursued through a given risk management effort must be understood if that effort is to have much chance of success. Such goals and objectives can come from the laws which guide DHS and its components (e.g., the Homeland Security Act of 2002 for DHS, Titles 14, 33 and 46 of the United States Code for the Coast Guard, the Transportation Security Act of 2001 for TSA, etc.) or from experience and knowledge of sound management practice (e.g., the need to guard against insider security threats).

Some goals and objectives apply across the board: safety of life, protection of property and the environment, sound fiscal stewardship, adherence to law and the Constitution, protection of civil liberties, etc.

Mission Space and Values

Defining roles & responsibilities in the service of your organization's goals and objectives.

Strategies, Policies, and Standards

Your risk management efforts should complement and take into account any risk management strategies, policies, standards, or requirements your organization has in place.

Scope and Criticality of the Decision

Not all risks are created equal. Some risks are of such magnitude that they justify significant expenditures of resources and require consideration of a wide range of possible courses of action, or even multiple courses of action. Others require far less investment. The breadth and scope of a given risk must be taken into account when deciding how to respond to it.

Decision Makers and Stakeholders

If you are the decision-maker/risk manager, it is probably a safe bet that you know your own decision-making style and information preferences and can describe them to your risk analyst. But if you are supporting the decision-maker/risk manager, you should identify and engage with that individual in order to better meet their preferences and expectations. Ideally, the decision-maker/risk manager will be appropriately involved throughout the process.

Similarly, stakeholders (those individuals or groups affected by the decision) should be appropriately engaged and represented throughout the risk management process.

Together, the decision-maker/risk manager and the stakeholders help determine the decision-making environment. Some risk management decisions are clear cut and non-controversial. Other times, making risk management decisions can be very difficult, politically or otherwise, due to the number of competing interests involved.

Decision Timeframe

The timeframe in which a decision must be made and executed will dictate the speed, depth, and rigor of the risk management effort. Strategic risks may involve large resource commitments and therefore justify taking sufficient time to do rigorous analysis to ensure a fully-informed decision. Tactical risks, on the other hand, may require very quick decisions in order to protect life or property. "Pre-thinking" hypothetical, time-sensitive, high consequence decisions, as is done in some contingency planning, can help to ensure that important factors don't get missed in time-critical situations.

Risk Management Capabilities and Resources

The staff, money, skill sets, knowledge levels, and other resources available for managing a given risk will be key factors in determining what can be done and should be identified early in the risk management process.

Risk Tolerance

Having perspective on an organization or a decision maker's risk tolerance will help shape the assessments and the development of risk management alternatives.

Identify Potential Risk

The second step of the DHS Risk Management Cycle is to identify potential risks. The basic question being asked in this step is, "What can happen?" The decision's context established in the previous step can help answer this question and determine what risks should be identified and assessed.

It is also helpful to think of potential risk in terms of "risk to" and "risk from".

- **"Risk to"** includes the elements affected by a risk, such as people, property, the environment, a geographic area, asset, or system in the homeland security context or mission, goals, effectiveness, and staffing in the organizational context.
- **"Risk from"** includes the source of the risk, such as the threat or hazard in the homeland security context or institutional failures, poor planning, or lack of resources in the organizational context.

It is valuable to make an effort to identify risks beyond those usually considered. Risks that are newly developing or emerging are useful to identify. Risks that are highly unlikely but have high consequences should also be identified and incorporated into the assessment, if possible. Remember that no process for identifying risks is going to capture every potential hazard, threat, scenario or unwanted outcome and there will always be things that happen that are unanticipated.

Potential Sources of Risk Information

It is important to gather the right information when identifying potential risk. You need to consider what type of data and information is available, the possible sources of that information, and how it can be used.

Consider the following sources of information:

- Reviewing Past Events
- Open Source Information
- Brainstorming
- Red or Blue Teaming
- Modeling and Methodology
- Expert Elicitation
- Scenarios

Reviewing Past Events

For known hazards that occur somewhat frequently, such as hurricanes on the Gulf Coast or blizzards in the upper Midwest, you can study relevant past events and historical records to ascertain information on potential risks.

Open Source Information

Open source information includes data obtained from the Internet, broadcast media, books, and periodicals.

Brainstorming

Brainstorming is a good way to generate new ideas about potential risks, which could later be assessed for quality. Having more diverse perspectives will be better.

Red or Blue Teaming

Red teams and blue teams are groups of experts put together to think about future risks and risk mitigation options. Red teams are groups which are assigned to put themselves in the mindset of the adversary for the purpose of planning attacks, while blue teams are encouraged to develop creative solutions for stopping attacks.

Modeling and Methodology

Analytical tools to assist in decision analysis when data are available.

Expert Elicitation

In the homeland security context, expert elicitation can be used to speak with subject matter experts to get ideas about potential risks.

Scenarios

A scenario is a hypothetical situation comprised of a hazard, an entity impacted by the hazard, and the associated consequences. Scenarios are useful constructs to think about hazards and conditions that could then feed into a risk assessment.

Assess and Analyze Risk

The purpose of the third step of the risk management cycle is to assess the risks you have identified in the previous step and analyze the results of the assessment. To help clarify this step, consider how you would answer these two basic questions.

- How likely is it that something will happen?
- If it does happen, what are the consequences?

The results of the assessment will enable you to develop risk management strategies in the next step of the cycle.

Tasks for Assessing and Analyzing Risk

Assessing and analyzing identified risks is a crucial step in the DHS Risk Management Cycle. It involves the following tasks:

- Determining a Methodology
- Gathering Data
- Validating and Verifying

Determining a Methodology

A risk assessment methodology is a set of methods, principles, or rules used to identify and assess risks in order to generate information needed to complete subsequent steps in the risk management cycle and to form priorities, develop courses of action, and inform decision-making. Some important factors to consider in selecting a risk assessment methodology are the characteristics of the risk in question (the hazard/threat, the entity at risk, and potential consequences) together with the characteristics of the decision the assessment must inform and the demands of the decision-making environment.

The methodology should only be as complex as necessary to properly inform subsequent steps in the risk management cycle and to satisfy the legitimate expectations of the decision-maker/risk manager and key stakeholders. Simple, but defensible, methodologies are usually preferred over more complicated methods. In some cases, such as tactical risk decisions made in the field, the risk assessment may be as informal and simple as a mental checklist being run through by, for example, a law enforcement officer about to enter a potentially dangerous situation. The need to be informal and even simple does not mean that the assessment can also be sloppily performed or incomplete. Most risk assessment methodologies assess risk in terms of their likelihood and consequences.

Gathering Data

Once a methodology for the risk assessment has been determined, data must be gathered. Sources of risk information are similar to those for identifying potential risks. They include historical records, models, simulations, and elicitations of subject-matter experts together with real-world observations of a situation on the ground.

Verifying and Validating

Throughout the execution of the risk assessment, gathered data, evidence, and results should be carefully studied and compared to previous works to ensure validity. Verification is the determination that a risk model works as intended. Validation involves determining whether the risk model provides reasonable results relative to observed or other modeled results.

The final task in performing a risk assessment is to ensure the results are ready for use in the following steps of the risk management cycle and for presentation to the decision-maker/risk manager.

Risk assessment results are not a decision-ready final product. They will provide arguments for development and evaluation of alternative courses of action and to support other follow-on analyses that may be required. Risk assessment results also provide information useful in supporting effective risk communications.

Risk Management in Real Life

Are you beginning to understand the role of risk management in decision-making? Look at the first step of the DHS Risk Management Cycle.

Think about how the context of decision-making for airport security has changed since September 11, 2001. We live in a very different environment since that time and our risk management has to reflect that.

Now, consider the second step. We at TSA identified the potential risk of someone carrying explosives on their person or in their luggage, using many of the methods described earlier.

When these were identified as potential sources of risk, we had to assess the risks in order to inform decisions about possible courses of action.

TSA used past events and intelligence information to assess the likelihood of these potential risks, and past events plus engineering studies to assess the consequences.

In the next lesson you'll learn more about developing and choosing from alternatives and implementing risk management decisions.

Lesson Summary

In this lesson you learned about the DHS Risk Management Cycle and how it is used.

The first three steps of the cycle are defining the context of a decision, identifying potential risk, and assessing and analyzing that risk. Within the third step, we recognize the likelihood and consequences of a particular risk.

By carefully following these steps, you are establishing a solid base for the risk management decisions and actions that will be reached by executing the remaining steps in the DHS Risk Management Cycle, as described in the following lessons.

Lesson 4: The DHS Risk Management Cycle (Part 2)

Lesson Overview

In this lesson you will learn about the last three steps in the DHS Risk Management Cycle. These crucial steps will help you understand how to develop alternatives for the risks you have identified and analyzed. A major part of this is choosing among different risk management strategies.

Further, you will learn about implementing a decision and the importance of evaluating and monitoring a situation after implementation.

Upon completion of this lesson, you will be able to:

- Define various strategies for managing risk.
- Identify methods for developing and evaluating risk management alternatives.
- Recognize the effect of risk perception on decision-making.
- Select an appropriate strategy for managing risk in a given scenario.

Risk Management in Real Life

We've talked some about the screening process in airports and how risk management decision-making is a big part of that.

One difficult aspect of risk management for TSA and many other organizations is that risks and the overall risk environment are always changing. So, having a risk management process to deal with those changes is vital.

In the DHS Risk Management Cycle, a key step is to develop alternative ways to manage a risk by choosing certain strategies.

As you read about the different risk management strategies, think about how they might apply to transportation security and we'll discuss this some more later.

Develop Alternatives: Risk Management Strategies

So far, we have covered the first three steps of the DHS Risk Management Cycle. After identified risks have been assessed, the next step of the risk management cycle is to develop potential risk management alternatives and determine their associated costs and benefits. These actions provide decision-makers/risk managers with a range of fully evaluated alternatives from which to choose.

There are two basic questions to be answered when developing and then evaluating alternatives.

- What could I do about it?
- What should I do about it?

Risk Management Strategies

The development of alternatives includes the use of risk management strategies. There are, in very general terms, four different ways of responding to risks. Choosing between strategies always involves "trade-offs." Frequently, these trade-offs involve accepting a smaller risk to avoid a larger one (e.g., accepting the risks associated with vaccination rather than the risk of contracting a potentially deadly disease) or accepting a smaller known cost in order to reduce a potentially larger unknown cost (e.g., accepting the actual cost of a flood prevention levy rather than the risk of a far more costly flood).

Risk Acceptance

Sometimes, the most appropriate or responsible action is to do nothing and accept the risk. Risk acceptance is an explicit or implicit decision to accept the consequences of a given risk.

Example: Instead of buying a backup generator, you decide to accept the risks associated with losing power in a storm.

Risk Avoidance

Risk avoidance is a strategy taken that effectively removes the exposure to a risk. With risk avoidance, a decision is made to either completely remove the sources of a particular risk or when an organization or individual remove themselves from a particular risk.

Example: You are at the beach and decide not to get in the water to avoid a chance of getting attacked by a shark.

Caution: Risk Avoidance can sometimes result in unknowing acceptance of an alternative, and possibly greater risk than the one avoided. For example, by deciding to make a long trip by car rather than by flying, due to the perceived risk of flying, a traveler will likely expose him or herself to a much greater risk of injury or death (statistically speaking).

Risk Control

Risk control, also known as risk reduction or risk mitigation, is the most common of the four strategy categories in the homeland security environment. Risk control is a strategy of deliberate actions taken to reduce the likelihood of a threat or hazard being experienced, to reduce the likelihood that damage will result should the hazard or threat be experienced, or to minimize harm once a hazard or threat has been experienced.

Example: Fans coming into a sporting event are screened with metal detectors and bag searches to reduce the likelihood of weapons or explosives entering the area. Another example would be a flood control levy built to limit or prevent flood damage.

Risk Transfer

Risk Transfer is a strategy of shifting some or all of the risk to another entity, asset, system, network, or geographic area. This can take several forms, including purchasing insurance and the kind of threat-shifting that occurs when terrorists choose an easier and less valuable target to hit. Risk transfer may not reduce the overall likelihood of a particular threat or hazard being experienced but it should make the consequences easier to bear.

Example: You purchase car insurance, thereby accepting the cost of your insurance premiums, in order to avoid having to pay the full cost of damage repairs to your vehicle.

Methods for Developing and Evaluating Alternatives

Developing alternative courses of action requires understanding the technical and/or operational measures that can either break the cause and effect linkage to likelihood or reduce the consequences that would result if a given hazard or threat were to be experienced. While every situation is unique, input from a variety of subject matter experts using a variety of methods can be used. These include:

- Reviewing lessons learned from relevant past incidents
- Consulting subject matter experts, best practices, and government guidelines
- Brainstorming
- Modeling and simulation
- Engineering experiments and field trials

Developing Alternatives: Costs and Benefits

Evaluating identified potential alternative courses of action requires developing realistic estimates or projections of the overall costs for each alternative together with the associated benefits. Costs, in this context, include not just the monetary cost of a course of action but also other costs such as degradation of civil liberties, other adverse political impacts, opportunity costs (i.e., alternative uses of time and money not possible due to a given course of action), and so forth.

In general, the benefits of a risk management action will consist of the consequences (or harm) reduced or avoided. Some courses of action will impact or go hand-in-hand with others. For example, selecting one course of action may require selection of a complementary course or present requirements for investing in supporting infrastructure, training, etc. that may not be initially apparent, thus lending to the value of performing a thorough analysis. In doing cost and benefit analyses, the costs and benefits should be aggregated over the full life-cycle of the various courses of action. This is particularly important for options whose up-front costs are only a fraction of their full life-cycle costs.

Once the full costs and benefits of potentially viable courses of action have been prepared, decision-makers/risk managers can be presented with the full picture of assessed risk, alternative courses of action, the costs and benefits associated with each and, if the decision-maker/risk manager so chooses, recommendations on the best course(s) of action.

Risk Perception in the DHS Risk Management Cycle

As discussed earlier, risk perception is an important factor in risk management. For one thing, it is the perception of risk that drives the call for some form of risk management action in the first place.

Moreover, risk perception plays an important role throughout various steps of the DHS Risk Management Cycle. When evaluating alternatives you might be much more likely to choose or recommend risk acceptance as a strategy if you perceive the likelihood of a risk as relatively low or its consequences as negligible. However, this perception might be wrong. This is why careful assessment and analysis are so central to properly carrying out the Risk Management Cycle.

It is imperative to both be aware of risk perceptions and to look beyond those perceptions to ensure that, to the maximum extent possible, decisions and actions are based on the best available factual basis.

Decide and Implement

Risk management entails making decisions about the best options from among a number of choices in an uncertain environment. The next step in the DHS Risk Management Cycle is to make and implement a decision. At this point in the cycle, the main question is, "What am I going to do (or not do) about it?"

The key moment in the execution of any risk management process is when a decision-maker chooses among alternatives for managing risks, and makes an informed decision to implement the selected course of action. Keep in mind that a leader can generally make two types of decisions: a decision to implement a new strategy or a conscious decision to maintain the status quo after considering other options.

Once a decision has been made, the decision maker must ensure that the decision is documented and communicated, and that an appropriate management structure is in place to implement the decision.

Implementing a risk management decision may be as simple as gathering the items deemed necessary for an evacuation, such as a "go-kit" or a shelter-in-place supply stash at home. However, at work it might involve developing and fielding an entire new operating program that requires personnel, equipment, or new operational doctrine and possibly extends over many years.

Evaluate and Monitor

The sixth and final step of the risk management cycle is to <u>evaluate</u> the adopted risk management strategy over time and to monitor both the risk and its context for changes that might require modifying, or even abandoning, the adopted risk management strategy and course of action.

Individuals and organizations both need to bse able to determine if their adopted risk management strategy is achieving the intended performance objective. Further, especially in the workplace, there is a need for organizations to be held accountable for their performance. Thus, it is crucial that a process of performance measurement be established.

In this final step of the risk management cycle, consider the following questions:

- How well is my chosen course of action working?
- Has anything changed that requires altering my existing risk management measures?
- Are there current trends and/or potential future developments that could require altering my existing risk management measures?

Evaluate

Modes of evaluation include internal review, external audit, red teaming, exercises, and after-action reports. Additionally, for every adopted risk management action there is an expectation that the action will create some identifiable positive benefit.

The value of testing the effectiveness of strategies using these methods is that it provides different perspectives on the success of the risk management approach and the capabilities of the organization.

Monitor

From "risk management fundamentals: "It is also important to monitor the larger context within which an identified risk and risk management effort exists. Good situational awareness may reveal changes in the context that require corresponding changes in the risk management effort. Both types of monitoring - effectiveness and situational awareness - are essential if risk management efforts are to be effective over time.

Questions Throughout the DHS Risk Management Cycle

Risk management allows us to do many things. At DHS, it enables us to distinguish between and among alternative actions, assess our capabilities, and prioritize activities and resources. In order to manage risk effectively, there are certain key principles that we must follow:

Let's review the steps of the DHS Risk Management Cycle that we have covered and how they fit together as a process for managing risk. Select each step in the cycle to see the basic questions you would answer in that step (Haimes, 1991; Kaplan and Garrick, 1981). This will help reinforce what you have already learned and emphasize the practical application of the cycle

Define the Context

These questions help you to understand what you should be concerned about and why.

- What are my risk management responsibilities?
- What is my risk management environment?
- What outcomes and objectives am I expected to achieve?

Identify Potential Risk

This question gets at the kinds of events or hazards that would affect the things you are concerned about.

- What can happen?

Assess and Analyze Risk

Answers to these questions give us information that helps determine if doing something is appropriate and provide the basis for deciding which course of action would be the most beneficial and cost-effective.

- How likely is it that something will happen?
- If it does happen, what are the consequences?

Develop Alternatives

Answering this first question requires that we understand the nature and cause of the risk in question as well as the technical, operational, or other ways of affecting the cause and effect relationship. The second question looks at the costs and benefits of the various options and provides the basis for a decision about what to do.

- What could I do about a risk?
- What should I do about a risk?

Decide and Implement

Once the information generated in the preceding questions is in hand, a decision can be made about which course of action, including the possibility of deliberately doing nothing, to adopt. Any decision to act must be followed by the actions required to implement it.

- What am I going to do to mitigate the impact of a risk?

Evaluate and Monitor

Once an adopted course of action has been implemented, including the action of deliberately doing nothing, good managers will keep tabs on the effectiveness of their actions. They will also be attentive to changes or potential changes in the programs and risks they are managing so that they can make necessary mid-course corrections. These questions help in meeting those managerial responsibilities.

- How well is my chosen course of action working?
- Has anything changed that requires altering my existing risk management measures?
- Are there current trends and/or potential future developments that require altering my existing risk management measures?

Communication

Effective communications is at the center of good risk management and plays a role at every step of the cycle. These questions help in identifying and satisfying risk communications needs.

- What risk information needs to be communicated?
- Between whom does it need to be communicated?
- How can necessary risk information be most effectively communicated?

Risk Management in Real Life

Were you able to think of how risk management strategies would apply to transportation security and the decisions we make at TSA? Consider risk acceptance. When it comes to traveling safely and securely on a train, bus, or airplane, most of us wouldn't be too comfortable with the idea of risk acceptance alone.

How about risk avoidance, or removing the exposure to a risk? That doesn't sound too bad but can we realistically remove all transportation risks? As a personal decision, one could choose not to fly and thereby remove themselves from that risk.

However, if we decide not to fly somewhere and drive instead, we are exposing ourselves to a new set of potentially greater risks, still with the likelihood of negative consequences.

As this lesson mentioned, risk control is the most common type of strategy chosen, in general, and that is also the case when it comes to transportation security or other security measures within DHS.

Airport screening is mostly about risk control and the idea of trying to minimize risks and maintain them at an acceptable level. Having varied and flexible measures for scanning decreases the risk of explosives being brought aboard a plane in someone's clothing or luggage, therefore maintaining that risk at an acceptable level.

However, notice the words "at an acceptable level" suggest an element of risk acceptance as well. Some of the most stringent security measures are applied only infrequently and under special circumstances. The risk might be even a little bit lower if these measures were applied to everyone, all the time.

However, it would be prohibitively expensive, disruptive to travel, and very intrusive. So, as often is the case, we've controlled a large part of the risk but chosen to accept some small remaining risk.

Another illustration we can make here relates to monitoring and evaluation. You might encounter a new airport screening method and then see that changed after a short time.

For example, a screening method to not allow certain objects through security was implemented early in TSA's history but has now been removed after further evaluation. Such changes and adjustments are an important part of the evaluation and monitoring process within the DHS Risk Management Cycle.

Regardless of how thorough any organization tries to be in its risk management decision-making, there is no guarantee that the outcomes of those decisions are going to be perfect. Still, by practicing sound risk management, we greatly improve the chances of making good decisions about appropriate and effective responses to identified risks.

Lesson Summary

The DHS Risk Management Cycle is a structured approach to risk management decision-making. A major part of this approach is the development of alternative courses of action for a set of identified risks which have been scrutinized through careful assessment and analysis.

With these alternatives in hand, decision-makers can choose and then implement one or more courses of action. The final step of the DHS Risk Management Cycle includes careful monitoring and evaluation of an adopted risk management strategy.

Lesson 5: Risk Communication

Lesson Overview

Throughout the DHS Risk Management Cycle one of the most important factors is communication. Effective risk communication brings cohesion to the decision-making process and ensures that objectives are being met at every step of the cycle.

Successful risk communication involves the knowledge of different types of communication as well as an understanding of many key considerations.

Upon completion of this lesson, you will be able to:

- Identify the role of risk communication in risk management.
- Describe how risk perception influences communication.
- Recognize characteristics and principles for effective risk communication.
- Identify examples of effective and ineffective risk communication.

Risk Management in Real Life

Hello, again. Are you familiar with the "If You See Something, Say Something TM" public awareness campaign launched by DHS in 2010? It is a program designed to raise awareness of the indicators of terrorism and violent crime, and to emphasize the importance of reporting suspicious activity to the proper local and state law enforcement authorities.

A key component of this public awareness campaign is enhancing effective communication between the public and authorities. We all know how important communication can be in many areas of our life. Well, it is no less important when it comes to risk management.

The "If You See Something, Say SomethingTM" campaign illustrates the need for effective communication when it comes to managing the risks of terrorism or violent crimes. The eyes of the public are valuable tools when it comes to identifying potential risks.

However, the average person needs to have an idea of what to look for and how to get that information to the proper authorities. Through this awareness campaign, DHS is attempting to educate the public and enhance this communication process in an effort to keep our nation safe.

Risk Communication

Risk communication is the exchange of information with the goal of improving risk understanding, affecting risk perception, and/or equipping people or groups to act appropriately in response to an identified risk.

Communications underpin the entire risk management process. Risk communication is a multidirectional process and should be ongoing throughout the life of a risk management action or strategy to ensure that everyone affected by either the risk or the risk management action will have the information they need at the time they need to have it.

Strong and effective communication is the foundation of the risk management process. For example, as part of a risk management process, an organization will maintain communication among team members, analysts, stakeholders, partners, and customers to keep a project or decision moving through the risk management process.

As with the other aspects of the Risk Management Cycle, there are a few basic questions that can help guide the Risk communications process. These are:

- What risk information needs to be communicated?
- Between whom does it need to be communicated?
- How can necessary risk information be most effectively communicated?

Information to Communicate

Information that needs to be communicated can include risk perceptions, factual information about a given threat or hazard, information about consequences, the results of risk assessments, alternative courses of action, and more. However, not everyone needs to have the same information.

For example, the general public probably does not need the details of assessments or risk management actions taken with respect to internal risks. On the other hand, the public will need information on topics such as how to prepare a "go kit" or evacuate a projected hurricane impact area. This pre-event information might come through resources like the Ready.gov website. After an event, necessary information will likely come from designated spokespersons making public announcements.

The people of the United States are so diverse in so many ways that no single communication mode will satisfy the needs of the entire population. By addressing that diversity and using appropriate methods to communicate the necessary information throughout the DHS Risk Management Cycle, it will be possible for people managing risks to develop and maintain effective risk communications plans.

Risk communication can be broken down into internal and external communication. It can also be divided into pre-decisional and post-decisional, as well as pre-event and post-event. Of course, those involved and the information communicated will change depending on the context.

Below are some examples of risk communication:

- Public addresses or alerts
- Warning systems
- Brochures or flyers (e.g., At health care facilities, the DMV, etc.)
- Television ads
- Public awareness campaigns (e.g., If You See Something, Say Something)
- Signs, videos, and announcements at the airport (particularly in the screening area)
- Briefs to leadership
- Emails/memos
- Reports
- Meetings at work
- Town hall meetings with the public

Internal Risk Communication

Internal communication can include communication that is between analysts and decision-makers, among subject matter experts, and across component organizations within DHS. Ensuring that information is received and shared is crucial to internal communications throughout the risk management cycle.

Being transparent about methodology, limitations, and uncertainty provides decision-makers with the most accurate, defensible, and practical information on which to base risk management decisions.

External Risk Communication

DHS employees often communicate with external stakeholders and partners (like other agencies or state and local governments) as well as the private sector and members of the public in order to better understand their perceptions of risk. Further, these external stakeholders frequently have extensive and superior knowledge which DHS should take advantage of as it begins to assess risk and develop risk management strategies. This cannot be done without effective two-way communications.

Other agencies and levels of government, as well as the public and the private sectors, often have important roles to play in reducing risk, making them an integral part of the risk management process. To fulfill these roles, other players must have information on what they need to do, as well as when, how, and why to do it.

U.S. Coast Guard team member:

So why is risk communication so important? First of all, it's conveying information that someone can use. But it's also a way to influence a person's thoughts about the information that he or she is receiving. We all receive information differently and we hear the information from our own perspectives.

So that means we superimpose our values on the message that is being sent. If we, as DHS, are hoping to help move the needle towards reducing risk, we can't do it alone. We need our partners to understand the risk and why implementing the measure we're asking them to do is important to them. It's the old adage of everyone listens to their favorite radio station, W-I-I-F-M or What's in it for me?

So how do we send a message that is consistent in its delivery and relates to how someone else might hear it? While there is no one or simple way to implement risk communication, you can consider the following aspects as you develop a script to convey your message as well as influence the way in which your message is heard.

- Do you have a credible basis for your position?
- Is there a regulation, statute or department policy that is driving your action?
- Have you identified the best way to communicate this message to your audience?
- Can you acknowledge and/or empathize that your customer might have a different point of view that has not yet been addressed?
- Can you compare this risk to other risks that they might know so that they can better comprehend the risk and the need to respond appropriately?

Incident-driven vs. Routine Communications

How risk communications are conducted can differ based on the relevance of time pressure, the purpose of the message, and the entity responsible for communicating the information.

Many types of risk communications are routine and involve little time pressure. Typically, routine risk communications are intended to inform and empower decision-making among partners, stakeholders, and the public and/or to influence risk perceptions with information based on fact rather than fear. Incident or emergency communications, however, take place under different conditions and impose very different demands on those responsible for getting the message out.

In an emergency, time constraints are a critical consideration and the need to explain and persuade becomes increasingly important as a result of psychological changes in how people take in and act on information and protective guidance.

One of the best ways to ensure effective emergency communications is to begin preparing the audience – frequently members of the public – to receive the message

BEFORE the emergency happens. This can be done by being open to communications, by providing information that is needed before an emergency, and by trying to build a reputation for credibility and competence. Waiting for an emergency to happen before doing these things will only guarantee failure.

Risk Communication and Risk Perception

As mentioned earlier, varying risk perceptions need to be taken into account when communicating. Risk perception influences a person's attitude towards risk, which then influences that person's behavior. Erroneous risk perceptions, if discovered in a timely manner through open communications, provide an educational target that can be addressed through subsequent risk communications efforts.

For example, the public might generally perceive a greater danger from shark attacks after a movie like "Jaws" is released. Perceptions that have been influenced by a recent event, or even by scary fiction such as the movie "Jaws," may be unrealistic and drive counterproductive responses to a misperceived risk resulting in untended and greater negative consequences. An example directly relevant to DHS is that, in the months after the September 11, 2001 attacks, an increase in the number of people choosing not to fly led to substantially more highway deaths." (Gigerenzer, 2006).

This is very important to keep in mind when considering risk communication; whether it is communication about a risk assessment or communications surrounding an incident or event. You need to account for the various risk perceptions of audiences and draft your communications to address those perceptions.

Risk Communication Considerations

Regardless of whether your audience is internal or external, there are several considerations for risk communication that you should think about while forming risk communication messages.

- Plan for Communications
- Build and Maintain Trust
- Use Language Appropriate to the Audience
- Be Both Clear and Transparent
- Respect the Audience's Concerns
- Maintain Integrity of Information

Additional information on risk communication can be found in the publication *Improving Risk Communication*, authored by the National Research Council Committee on Risk Perception and Communication and published in 1989.

Plan for Communications

Communication needs to be part of the risk management process; it should not be an afterthought. The information needs of different audiences will vary depending on circumstances, but risk information needs to be available for all stakeholders throughout the risk management cycle.

It is important that these plans include opportunities for two-way communication

Build and Maintain Trust

Past communication efforts will affect future efforts, especially if they are related to the same situation. How your message is received will depend on how previous messages were given and received.

Maintaining consistency is important but not at the expense of accuracy. If new information is not consistent with what you've said in the past, then you need to acknowledge the change or previous mistakes and then explain the situation as it stands.

For example, this would hold true if you are an analyst who is modifying your assessment results based on new data or if you are a public official providing new informsation about an industrial disaster and either the situation has changed or new facts have come into the possession of the authorities.

Use Language Appropriate to the Audience

Consider who your audience is and make sure the language and type of communication is tailored to them. Be aware of those who may speak other languages and make accommodations for individuals with access and functional needs as well.

Make sure that the information is conveyed in a way that leads to your organization's desired actions and outcomes. Is your audience DHS leadership? Are they state and local partners or the general public? The way you convey the message will vary for each of these audiences.

Be Both Clear and Transparent

Clarity means communicating in a direct, simple and understandable way. Avoiding jargon and discussing the situation without technical or scientific information, unless it is necessary for the audience, are other examples of ways to ensure your communication is clear. Transparency means disclosing assumptions, methodologies, and uncertainties.

Respect the Audience's Concerns

Acknowledge the audience's concerns and/or issues and provide them with opportunities for collaboration or providing feedback when possible. It's important as a risk communicator to answer questions and provide options. If you say you are going to get back to someone, make sure you follow up. And remember that those you are communicating with may have important information that you don't have, or may have important concerns of which you are unaware.

Maintain Integrity of Information

Acknowledge uncertainty, note limitations of the data, discuss assumptions, and distinguish between results that are and are not supported by analysis.

Risk Management in Real Life

As you can see, communication is an important part of risk management. I know how vital it is for my own job.

Whether it is part of a formal risk management process or just within the routine of normal duties, I understand the need for all parties to be as informed as possible and how that can only happen through active communication.

I hope that some of the things we have talked about today have helped you to better understand risk management. Risk management is obviously an essential part of my job. As a transportation security officer, I'm working to help keep people secure from risks.

Even if you haven't thought much about risk management in your job, I'm guessing that you can see now that these ideas have valuable application in every workplace.

We also talked about how risk management plays a role in our communities and in our homes. Maybe you'll start thinking about some of the decisions you make at home and how you go about applying risk management to those.

You might also be a little more aware of actions being taken about particular risks in your community and how you can contribute to those efforts. At the end of the day, we all stand to benefit from effective use of risk management principles in dealing with issues at work and at home.

Lesson Summary

In this lesson you have learned about the significance of effective communication throughout the DHS Risk Management Cycle.

Communication must be a planned part of your overall risk management effort as opposed to an afterthought. Both internal and external communication work to keep risk management moving forward and to ensure that everyone is involved and working toward the same goals. Effective communication has the power to establish a positive and productive environment based on trust, respect, transparency, and integrity.

Course Summary

Risk management is a part of DHS culture and a vital part of our ongoing effort to protect the Nation from a diverse and complex set of threats and hazards. Through this course you learned about the essential role of risk management at home, in the community, and in your workplace. As part of the DHS workforce, it is critical that you understand the fundamentals of risk management and how those might apply to your roles and responsibilities.

While risk management can inform decision making, in the final analysis, it is really what we do to manage risk that matters. The DHS Risk Management Cycle provides a sound approach for applying the principles and concepts of risk management to decision-making and operations. With these tools and knowledge, you stand poised to provide a greater contribution to the risk management efforts at DHS.